COUNT ON ME
orts

Inspiring Stori...
SPORTSMANSHIP

BRAD HERZOG

"As shown by the wonderful stories in
Count on Me: Sports, athletics can not only
reveal character, but also inspire it."
—**Shannon Miller**, two-time Olympic gold medalist
in gymnastics

"The true tales in Brad Herzog's books
show how the games we play can teach
seriously important life lessons."
—**Jake Delhomme**, former Super Bowl quarterback
for the Carolina Panthers

free spirit
PUBLISHING®

Library of Congress Cataloging-in-Publication Data
Herzog, Brad.
 Inspiring stories of sportsmanship / Brad Herzog.
   pages cm. — (Count on me: sports)
 Includes index.
 Summary: "Teaches kids about positive character and sportsmanship through real-life examples."
 ISBN-13: 978-1-57542-455-2 (pbk.)
 ISBN-10: 1-57542-455-X
 1. Sportsmanship—Juvenile literature. I. Title.
 GV706.3.H47 2014
 175—dc23   2013045283

eBook ISBN: 978-1-57542-600-6

Reading Level Grade 5; Interest Level Ages 8–13;
Fountas & Pinnell Guided Reading Level T

Edited by Alison Behnke
Cover and interior design by Michelle Lee Lagerroos

Cover photo credits: background © Bruxov | Dreamstime.com; clockwise from top left:
AP Photo/David J. Phillip; AP Photo/Blake Wolf; AP Photo/Paul Sancya;
Press Association via AP Images; AP Photo/Frank Gunn/CP; AP Photo/Alastair Grant.
For interior photo credits, see page 94.

10 9 8 7 6 5 4 3 2 1
Printed in the United States of America
S18860214

Free Spirit Publishing Inc.
Minneapolis, MN
(612) 338-2068
help4kids@freespirit.com
www.freespirit.com

DEDICATION

In memory of Court Erickson, who never lost his youthful enthusiasm, his love of sports, or his generosity of spirit.

ACKNOWLEDGMENTS

Thank you to Judy Galbraith, Margie Lisovskis, and the rest of the crew at Free Spirit Publishing for having the courage to pursue a series of books celebrating stories of character in sports. I found Alison Behnke to be both insightful and inclusive as an editor, an author's dream combination, and Michelle Lee Lagerroos put in overtime making sure the designs were just right. Finally, I am grateful to Aimee Jackson for bringing me to Free Spirit in the first place and for her unwavering support and friendship.

CONTENTS

INTRODUCTION

Sportsmanship takes many different forms. That can make it tough to define. Sportsmanship can mean winning fairly, competing with integrity, or losing with dignity. It can mean showing humility or honesty, or sticking to your values even during fierce competition. Someone might show sportsmanship by helping a fallen opponent, or by sacrificing to help someone else. It can take place on the field, in the stands, or far from the action. It can be demonstrated by players, coaches, referees, or fans. It can happen during a game or before a match or even long afterward. Whatever form it takes, we know true sportsmanship when we see it.

The author Mark Twain had his own humorous thoughts on the idea. "It's good sportsmanship," he once noted, "to not pick up lost golf balls while they are still rolling." Of course, most of us prefer to aim a bit higher than that. Bobby Jones certainly did.

Many people view Bobby Jones as the best amateur golfer in history. He was a seven-time major golf

1

champion. And he was nearly as well known for being a sportsman as he was for being a champ. During the 1925 U.S. Open, Jones hit a poor shot. His ball landed in the rough (the taller grass next to the main fairway). As he was getting ready to take his next shot, his club bumped the ball, moving it slightly. That's against the rules. But nobody had seen it happen. Not the course marshals, who had the job of applying those rules. Not the fans standing nearby. Nobody but Bobby Jones.

Jones told the marshals about his mistake. Because no one else actually saw it happen, the officials said that Jones could decide what to do. He didn't hesitate. He called a two-stroke penalty against himself. He later lost the tournament—by a single stroke. Today, the United States Golf Association's sportsmanship honor is named the Bob Jones Award. But after the tournament, when people praised Jones for his gesture, he just shrugged his shoulders and replied, "You may as well praise a man for not robbing a bank."

What Jones was saying was: Why expect anything less? Shouldn't good sportsmanship be the rule, not the exception?

Yet great acts of sportsmanship can inspire us all. At about the same time Bobby Jones was dominating the golf world, a man by the name of Knute Rockne was dominating college football. Rockne coached the University of Notre Dame team, and he led them to five undefeated seasons. Rockne once said, "One man practicing good sportsmanship is far better than 50 others preaching it."

This book is full of stories of people practicing good sportsmanship. It features athletes and coaches in everything from football and fencing to soccer, sailing, tennis, and tae kwon do. This is a book about winners—even when they didn't win.

CARRYING ON

APRIL 26, 2008 • ELLENSBURG, WASHINGTON, UNITED STATES

On a beautiful spring afternoon, a five-foot-two-inch right fielder made the swing of her life. The setting was a softball game between rivals Central Washington University and Western Oregon University. Western's Sara Tucholsky had a poor batting average of .153. She had never hit a home run—not even in batting practice. Then, in the second inning she smashed the ball over the center field fence. With two players on base, it would be a three-run shot. Thrilled, Tucholsky sprinted toward first base. But as she watched the ball clear the fence, she missed first base. When she stopped quickly to go back and touch it, something in her knee gave out. She fell to the ground.

In terrible pain, Tucholsky crawled through the dirt back to first base. The Western coach rushed onto the field. The umpires told the coach it was against

the rules for Tucholsky's Western teammates to help her around the bases. The coach *could* substitute a runner for her. But then the hit would be judged a single. The only home run of Tucholsky's four-year career would be erased. The coach didn't know what to do.

That's when Mallory Holtman stepped in.

Holtman played first base for the other team. She was also Central Washington's all-time home run leader. She knew that if her team lost the game, their playoff hopes would probably be gone. But after listening to the coach and umpire for a while, she asked a question. *Can we do it? Is the other team allowed to carry her around the bases?*

The umpires said there was nothing in the rule book against it. So Holtman and Central's shortstop, Liz Wallace, walked over and helped Tucholsky up. Carrying her, they resumed the home run walk. At each base, they paused to let Tucholsky touch the bag with her uninjured leg. At second base, Holtman said, "I wonder what this must look like to other people."

The three players burst out laughing. The other people in the stadium weren't laughing, though. They were crying. The Western Oregon team, the coaches, and members of the crowd were shedding tears at seeing such a moving act of sportsmanship.

Tucholsky's Western team ended up winning the game 4 to 2. Afterward, someone realized that the umpires had made a mistake. The rules *did* allow a substitute runner, after all. But it didn't really matter. Character had triumphed.

"In the end, it's not about winning and losing so much," said Holtman. "It was about this girl. She hit it over the fence and was in pain. And she deserved a home run."

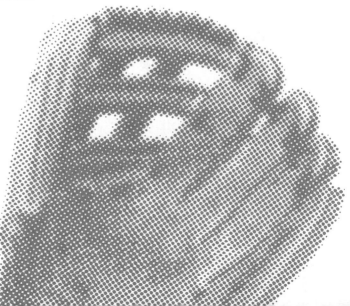

MILE MARKER

MARCH 11, 1956 • MELBOURNE, AUSTRALIA

In 1954, Englishman Roger Bannister became the first person to run a mile in under four minutes. Forty-six days later, Australian John Landy became the second. Landy also recorded a world record time of 3:57.9. So in August 1954, the world's two fastest milers faced off against each other. The competition was billed as "The Miracle Mile." More than 100 million people listened to the race over the radio. Millions more watched it on television. On the final turn of the last lap, Bannister passed Landy to win.

Still, Landy was an Australian sports hero. And in 1956, he also emerged as a hero of a different kind.

At the 1956 Australian National Championships, Landy was aiming to set another world record. The race was held at Olympic Park Stadium in the city of Melbourne. Landy was also trying to qualify for the Olympic Games that were to be held in Australia that summer. One of his fellow racers was 19-year-old Ron Clarke. Clarke was a world junior champion and would go on to set many records himself.

As the third of four laps began, a runner clipped Clarke's heel. Clarke tripped and fell onto the track. Landy, trailing close behind, tried to leap over him. In the process, his shoe's spikes scraped Clarke's arm. Landy had a choice. He could chase down a world record or stop to check on an injured friend. He chose to stop. With other runners streaming past him, Landy ran back to Clarke. He helped him to his feet, checked his bloodied arm, and apologized. "Keep going!" Clarke shouted. "I'm all right. Run!"

"For a moment I thought, *I've been disqualified*. Then I thought, *No, I'm still in the race*," Landy later recalled. "It looked impossible, with the rest of the field some 30 yards ahead, but I thought I'd better have a go."

Although he was far behind the rest of the field, he sprinted nearly the last half-mile. Every stride brought him closer to the leaders. To the delight of 22,000 spectators, Landy passed the two front runners in the last 10 yards. He won the race in a time of 4 minutes, 4.2 seconds. If he hadn't stopped to check on Clarke, he likely would have set a new world record.

Over 40 years later—not long before Landy became governor of the Australian state of Victoria—the Sport

Australia Hall of Fame voted on the nation's finest sporting moments. For the moment of the 20th century, they chose Landy's famous race. The voters weren't only celebrating the runner's remarkable final kick to win. They were also honoring his instinct to stop and help a competitor when stopping is the last thing a miler wants to do. In fact, a bronze sculpture of Landy now stands in Melbourne. It shows not the moment that Landy broke the tape to win the race, but rather the moment when he helped his fallen friend to his feet. The sculpture has a one-word title: "Sportsmanship."

SWELL GUY

DECEMBER 25, 1996 • SOUTHERN OCEAN

English sailor Pete Goss and French sailor Raphaël Dinelli had met just once, for a brief moment. The two were about to compete against each other. Along with other sailors, they were taking part in the 1996 Vendée Globe round-the-world yacht race. The event, held every four years, is one of the ultimate tests in ocean racing. In fact, some experts even say that more people have orbited Earth in space capsules than

12

have sailed solo around the world without help! On the morning the race would begin, Goss hopped onto Dinelli's boat and wished him luck. Dinelli spoke little English. The two men hardly knew each other. But their fates would soon collide.

Each yacht in the race had a special "mayday" button. A sailor would only push that button in a life-threatening situation. The button sent out a signal to race officials and rescue teams. Fifty days into the competition, on Christmas Day, Goss was sailing in the Southern Ocean. It was a cold and dangerous stretch of water where few ships ever ventured. Suddenly, he picked up a mayday signal in his cockpit.

The unfortunate sailor was Dinelli. An enormous storm had capsized his yacht. His mast broke, tearing a huge hole in the boat. After pushing the distress alarm, Dinelli had been lucky to make his way to the top of his boat. He clung there, hanging on through massive waves in bitterly cold temperatures. He had no food, and his feet were rapidly freezing. Soon they would go numb. When an Australian Air Force plane arrived, rescuers managed to drop a life raft. But the storm was so violent that an aircraft couldn't come any closer. Dinelli climbed into the raft just minutes before his boat sank. Now he could only wait, hoping that somebody might save him.

Goss was 160 miles away when he got the mayday signal. He had spent years preparing for this race. He had a wife and children at home, and he would be heading toward danger by going to help. It would take him dozens of hours to sail through the brutal storm toward Dinelli. But he was also the closest competitor who knew that his fellow sailor was in trouble. "It was up to me," Goss recalled.

SAILING SAVIOR

Canadian sailor Lawrence Lemieux was having a great race. He was in second place during a competition at the 1988 Summer Olympics in South Korea. Then he spotted two sailors in trouble. A team from Singapore, sailing in a different race, had capsized in strong winds. One man was hurt and floating away in open water. The other was clinging to the upside-down boat. Lemieux abandoned his chances of an Olympic medal and saved the two men. He finished his competition in 21st place, but he got a medal anyway. He won the Pierre de Coubertin medal, awarded for sportsmanship at the Olympics. "Hundreds of Olympic medals have been handed out over the years," Lemieux said. "But there haven't been too many for sportsmanship. I guess that's something to be proud of."

Goss's boat, the *Aqua Quorum*, toppled more than once in the hurricane-force winds. But he righted it and sailed toward his competitor. It took him 48 hours to arrive at Dinelli's position, and he finally spotted him bobbing in the life raft. Goss brought the Frenchman on board the *Aqua Quorum*. He nursed Dinelli back to health, giving him medicine and food and tea, warming his frozen feet, even carrying him to the bathroom.

In the process, the two men learned to communicate with each other and became close friends.

Goss went on to complete the race. He was one of only six sailors to do so, out of 16 who started. It took him nearly 127 days, which earned him only a fifth-place finish. But France awarded him the Légion d'honneur for his bravery. And Dinelli met him at the finish line.

The men later sailed together in a transatlantic race. But before that, Dinelli, having lived through his terrifying ordeal, asked his girlfriend to marry him. He asked his new friend Goss to be his best man.

ONE STEP BEHIND

For nearly three miles, 16-year-old Jenna Huff had been staring at 17-year-old Deb Guthmann's back. But when it mattered most, Huff *had* Guthmann's back.

The two were competing at a high school regional cross-country meet in North Carolina. Guthmann was a senior at Cuthbertson High School. Huff was a sophomore at North Stanly High. For much of the five-kilometer race, Guthmann had been anywhere from 10 to 40 yards ahead of Huff. The two runners were far from the lead. Their competition within a competition was still very important, though. Because their teams were tied in points for the season, the winning girl's school would be able to compete in the state tournament. The other school's team would not.

As they came within sight of the finish line, Huff was closing the gap with a strong finishing kick. As they ran through a sea of cheering spectators—parents, teammates, coaches, fans—she was about five yards behind Guthmann. There were 50 yards to go. Then she saw Guthmann grab her hip and cry out in pain.

A FRIENDLY PUSH

Meghan Vogel, a runner for West Liberty-Salem High School in Ohio, was tired. She had just won the 2012 state championship in the 1,600-meter race. She was so exhausted afterward that she was in last place toward the end of her next race, the 3,200 meters. As she came around the final turn in the long race, the runner in front of her, Arden McMath, fell to the ground. Vogel made a split-second decision. She stopped, helped McMath to her feet, and put her arm around her. Together, they walked the last 30 meters. Vogel guided McMath to the finish line. And then she gave McMath a gentle nudge across it, just ahead of Vogel herself. "If you work hard to get to the state meet, you deserve to finish," she said. "I was going to make that happen for her no matter what." Later, Vogel's hometown held a parade in her honor. It wasn't because of the race where she finished first. It was because of the race where she finished last.

Guthmann's hip had started to hurt halfway through the race. Now the pain was extreme. A piece of cartilage had popped off her hip. It was as painful as if she had broken a bone. She stopped, tears running down her face, just as Huff appeared at full sprint on her left.

Huff's first reaction was disbelief. *She ran three miles that fast*, she thought, *and she's going to stop right there? Right at the finish line?* For most runners, their next thought would be about themselves. After running hard for 20 minutes, why not run for a few seconds more?

Runners are taught to always pass slower rivals. Finish the race strong. But that's not what went through Jenna Huff's mind. "I didn't think about passing her," she said. "It wouldn't have been right, because she was hurt."

Instead, she gently grabbed Guthmann by the elbow. She said, "C'mon. We're going to run, and we're going to do it now." For the next 50 yards, she guided Guthmann, whom she had never met, to the finish line, step by step. "C'mon," she kept telling her. "Look, it's right there."

At the very end, it was Huff who stopped. She let Guthmann cross the line first. Cuthbertson High would be going to the state tournament. "She deserved to be in front of me," Huff explained. "She would have beaten me if she hadn't gotten hurt."

Most of the spectators who witnessed the event were teary-eyed. The father of another competitor told Huff that what she did was the best thing he had ever seen. Meanwhile, race officials huddled to make a decision. Technically, no runner is allowed to help another runner. But they decided to let the results stand. Guthmann finished in 21st place. Huff was 22nd—one second behind.

"I've never seen anything like it," said Guthmann's coach, David Malady. "Kids are always falling apart at or near the finish line—sick, tired, whatever. And they just get passed. Over and over. You just don't stop and grab somebody and help them. It's like an unwritten rule. You just don't. But Jenna did."

To show his thanks, Malady invited Huff to Cuthbertson's fall athletics banquet. Huff got a standing ovation from the crowd and a Cuthbertson varsity letter. She also got a big hug from Guthmann.

ACCEPTING IMPERFECTION

JUNE 2, 2010 • DETROIT, MICHIGAN, UNITED STATES

Sometimes the finest sporting gesture is a simple act of forgiveness.

In the spring of 2010, Jim Joyce had been a major league umpire for more than two decades. He was a widely respected baseball official. His skills had been tested during two World Series and a couple of

All-Star Games. Then, during a 2010 game between the Detroit Tigers and Cleveland Indians, he made a split-second decision. It didn't seem that different from hundreds he'd made during his career. But it would become the most important call of his career.

And he blew it.

It *should* have been the last play of the game. Pitching for Detroit was 28-year-old Armando Galarraga. Until then, he wasn't very well known outside Detroit. But now he was trying to pitch the 21st perfect game in baseball history. No base hits, no runs, no errors. Only 20 other major league players had ever accomplished the feat. And no Detroit pitcher had ever done it. Galarraga had already retired 26 batters in a row. With two men out in the ninth inning, there was just one more to go.

Cleveland's Jason Donald hit a ground ball between first and second base. Detroit first baseman Miguel Cabrera fielded it and tossed it to Galarraga, who had run over to cover first base. The pitcher caught the ball and touched the base—at least a full step ahead of the runner.

The thrilled crowd prepared to erupt in celebration. After all, they had just witnessed a piece of history. Detroit players raised their arms and got ready to rush from the dugout. The replays showed that Donald was clearly out. But Joyce, umpiring at first base, firmly called him safe.

The fans groaned. They booed the call mercilessly. Players argued. Detroit manager Jim Leyland was furious. He charged out of the dugout toward the umpire. Galarraga only smiled sadly at Joyce and walked back to the mound. Eventually, when the arguing stopped, he retired the next batter. The Tigers won the game 3–0. But in terms of baseball immortality, a one-hitter is far from perfection.

When the moment happened, Joyce was convinced that the runner had beaten the throw. However, when he watched a replay afterward he realized he had made a huge mistake. It was an error that would likely haunt him forever. But he took the brave step of unflinchingly admitting it. "I just cost that kid a perfect game," he despaired. Then he took the unusual step of asking for a chance to say he was sorry. He made his way to Detroit's locker room. With tears in

WISE WORDS

"In sport, part of the game is accepting the umpire's call, no matter how hard that might be. Sometimes the calls go your way, and sometimes they don't."
—Dr. Dot Richardson, former Olympic softball star

his eyes, he hugged Galarraga and apologized to him. Galarraga hugged him back. Later Galarraga told reporters, "You don't see an umpire after the game come out and say, 'Hey, let me tell you I'm sorry.' He felt really bad."

That heartfelt gesture made the pitcher, the manager, the team, and even a city full of disappointed fans feel a whole lot better. The next day, perfection wasn't the goal. Instead, it was forgiveness. It was Joyce's turn to umpire behind home plate. Leyland made the unusual move of having a player bring out the lineup card to the umpiring crew before the game. He wanted Galarraga to do it, and to shake hands with Joyce again. Leyland wanted the fans to see that the team understood a simple fact: Anyone can make an honest mistake.

The Tigers' third baseman Brandon Inge, had watched from the dugout. Later he said, "That was one of the coolest things I've ever seen. What sets that apart from anything that's probably happened in a long time in our sport is the absolute sportsmanship of it." Inge went on, "Galarraga and Joyce are two true gentlemen, period, in the way that they handled themselves. People will always remember that."

About a year after that memorable game, Joyce and Galarraga wrote a book together. The title? *Nobody's Perfect*.

THE FIFTH DOWN

NOVEMBER 16, 1940 • HANOVER, NEW HAMPSHIRE, UNITED STATES

In 1940, Cornell University had a powerhouse football team. Located in Ithaca, New York, Cornell's Big Red had won 18 straight games. They were ranked number two in the whole nation. In November, the team took a train to New Hampshire to face off against the lower-ranked team from Dartmouth College. It was a cold and snowy weekend. Dartmouth's Memorial Field was a muddy mess, leading to a sloppy game in front of the 8,000 fans who had braved the freezing temperatures. Neither team could move the ball much on the slushy field. The score sat at 0–0 until Dartmouth kicked a late field goal for three points. It looked like Cornell's winning streak might slip away.

Cornell had time for one last drive. They made it all the way to the six-yard line. A run on first down got them to the three-yard line. Another run moved the ball to the one-yard line. Then, on third down, Cornell players thought they had scored. But the referee didn't signal a touchdown. Cornell called a timeout, but they didn't have any left. So Red Friesell, one of the country's most respected referees, called a five-yard penalty. On fourth down, from just over the five-yard line, Cornell quarterback Walter Scholl threw an incomplete pass.

The game should have been over. Dartmouth was supposed to take possession. However, the unusual penalty had confused Friesell (along with many of

THE WRONG CHOICE

Half a century after the famous Cornell-Dartmouth football game, there was another fifth-down incident. It, too, happened on a sloppy, slippery playing field. October 6, 1990, the University of Colorado beat Missouri 33–31. But Colorado had mistakenly been given an extra down on the game's final play. Colorado coach Bill McCartney, a former Missouri player, was asked afterward if he would forfeit the game. He refused. Instead, he just complained that "the field was lousy." It was only years later, after he retired, that McCartney changed his mind. He said he was "truly remorseful" about what had happened.

the players). He mistakenly awarded Cornell one more play. With time about to run out, Scholl passed the ball to halfback Bill Murphy in the end zone. Touchdown! Final score: Cornell 7, Dartmouth 3. Back on the Cornell campus, the chimes in the clock tower rang out a song: "Cornell Victorious." The winning streak was saved.

Or was it?

Following the game, Dartmouth players insisted Cornell had scored only after being given an extra down. Many writers in the press box agreed. Both teams had filmed the game, so afterward Friesell watched the plays. He soon saw his mistake. Right away, Friesell sent a telegram to Dartmouth. It began, "I want to be the first to admit my very grave error . . ." In New York, the Cornell team came to the same conclusion after watching the game film. They *had* been given an undeserved fifth down.

Cornell coach Carl Snavely and university president Edmund Ezra Day huddled together and came to a decision: Either they win fairly, or not at all. Even though a national championship was on the line for the Big Red, Day sent a telegram to Dartmouth. He offered to forfeit the game. Dartmouth's coach accepted the offer. So the *real* final score was

Dartmouth 3, Cornell 0. It was the first time a college football game had ever been decided off the field.

Day gathered the Cornell football team together to tell them his decision. He said, "We have done the right thing, and this will live with us. We shall not have to spend the rest of our lives apologizing for a tarnished victory."

And what about the referee who made the fateful error? He was applauded for taking full responsibility. Friesell even got a telegram of his own from Asa Bushnell, head of the Eastern Football Association. It read: "Don't let this get you down . . . down . . . down . . . down . . . down."

LONG FRIENDSHIP

AUGUST 4, 1936 • BERLIN, GERMANY

The great Jesse Owens was in trouble. The American track and field star was the sensation of the 1936 Summer Olympics in Germany. But now he was one jump away from disaster. To qualify for the long jump semifinals, all he had to do was jump 23 feet, 5½ inches on at least one of his three tries. He had been doing that since high school. No problem.

Except there *was* a problem.

Owens, still in his warm-up clothes, had taken a practice jump. He didn't think it would count as an attempt. But an official had shocked him by ruling that it *did* count. The official also said that Owens had committed a foul by stepping over the line. Now nervous and upset, Owens tried again—and fouled again. If he made just one more mistake, his Olympic long jump hopes would be gone.

That's when he felt a tap on his shoulder. He turned to see Carl Ludwig "Luz" Long, a tall, strong

31

22-year-old. Long was a member of the German team, and he was the finest long jumper in Europe. He had easily qualified for the semifinals already. Now he told Owens, "You know, you should be able to qualify with your eyes closed." Then he offered some advice. Why not draw a mark a few inches *behind* the foul line, and take off from there? That mark would help prevent him from fouling. And with his ability, he should still qualify with inches to spare.

FRIENDLY ADVICE

American Bob Van Osdel and Canadian Duncan McNaughton attended college together at the University of Southern California. While they were there, Van Osdel informally coached McNaughton in track and field. To their surprise, at the 1932 Summer Olympics in Los Angeles, they wound up facing each other in the high jump final. Before the final, Van Osdel's advice to his friend was, "Get your kick working." It was enough to give McNaughton the edge. He won the gold medal. In a strange twist, the medal was stolen the next year. Van Osdel, by then a dentist, simply made a mold of his silver medal. Then he poured gold into the mold and sent the replica to his pal.

So Owens tried it. The result? He jumped more than 25 feet. Long came over and patted him on the back. "See," said the German, "it was easy." Owens smiled and clasped his hand. "Danke," he said. It was the only German word he knew. "Thank you."

Owens would go on to win the gold medal in the event, out-jumping Long in the finals. Luz Long immediately ran to congratulate him. In front of nearly 100,000 spectators—including German chancellor Adolph Hitler—Long threw his arm around Owens's shoulder and turned to the side of the stadium where Hitler was seated. Then he took Owens's hand in his, and raised it in triumph.

The long jump was one of four events in which Owens grabbed the gold at the Berlin Games. It was one of the most dominating performances in Olympic history. But Owens later said that Long's simple sporting gesture was the defining moment of his Olympic experience.

Why? Because the 1936 Olympics were about more than sports. At that time, Hitler and his followers were fueling racial and ethnic hatred in Germany. Hitler said that white Europeans were superior to all other people. Eventually his beliefs led to the murder of millions of Jewish people and others he considered inferior. Hitler had expected the Olympics to prove the superiority of white athletes—especially Germans. But one African American had defeated them all.

As for Owens and Long, they became close friends. They stayed in touch even during World War II, when Long was in the German Army that fought bitterly against the United States. In 1943, just a few days after communicating with Owens, Long was killed in the Battle of San Pietro. But Owens never forgot him. "It took a lot of courage for him to befriend me in front of Hitler," he said. "You can melt down all the medals and cups I have, and they wouldn't be a plating on the 24-karat friendship that I felt for Luz Long at that moment."

TOUCHING TRUTHFULNESS

AUGUST 4, 1932 • LOS ANGELES, CALIFORNIA, UNITED STATES

Fencing, a combat contest using swords, is one of the world's oldest sports. Some of history's most famous figures, including George Washington and Napoleon Bonaparte, enjoyed fencing. It is also one of only four sports to have been part of every modern Olympic Games since 1896. Two European nations, France and Italy, have been the most successful. Each country has earned more than 40 gold medals and more than 100 total Olympic medals in fencing over the years.

As for England . . . well, British fencers haven't had quite as much success. They have earned fewer than a dozen total medals. That's in spite of the fact that William Shakespeare—one of the most famous Brits of all—was probably the first person who described swordsmanship as "fencing."

So at the 1932 Summer Olympics in Los Angeles, Heather Guinness was trying to make history. She hoped to be the first-ever British gold medalist in fencing. Her chance came during a *barrage* (fence-off) for first place. It was 10 days before her 22nd birthday.

The sport of fencing is divided into three weapons: the epee, the sabre, and the foil. The epee is the heaviest of the three blades, and the foil is the lightest. Female Olympian fencers now compete in all three weapon categories. But until 1996, foil fencing was the only event in Olympic women's fencing.

In foil fencing, competitors must score "touches." A touch happens when a fencer hits her opponent using the tip of the foil's blade. The foil can touch the opponent's torso, including the back, but not the arms. Fencers wear special gear to protect their bodies.

In the summer of 1932, the two best female foil fencers in the world were Heather Guinness and Austria's Ellen Preis. Each woman came through the tournament with eight wins and only one loss. The next step was their barrage against each other. The winner would take home the top prize. In the previous two Summer Olympics, British fencers Gladys Davis (in 1924) and Muriel Freeman (in 1928) had earned silver medals. Guinness hoped to beat Preis and take home the gold.

Fencing is a very fast sport. The movements are often subtle. Blink, and you might miss a touch. These days, judges use an electrical scoring system. It lights up when a fencer successfully touches an opponent. But in 1932, these tools didn't exist yet. All judges could do was watch—*very* carefully. What they saw between Guinness and Preis was a closely fought match. In fact, it was so close that it seemed to be even. In the end, the fence-off came down to one factor—integrity. During the bout, Guinness pointed out a touch by her opponent that the judges had missed. Later, she did it again. Those two instances of honesty were enough to decide the victory. Preis won 5–3.

Guinness had lost the gold medal she'd dreamed of. But she had won fans throughout the world.

UPLIFTING HONESTY

At the 1948 Summer Olympics in London, England, American weightlifter Stanley Stanczyk appeared to have set a new world record. He had just hoisted 132.5 kilograms (about 292 pounds). The judges signaled that it was a fair lift. But Stanczyk shook his head and tapped his leg. He was saying that his knee had scraped the floor. The lift was no good. Despite the miss, he still went on to win the gold medal.

UNCONTESTED GOAL

At first it seemed like a typical game of soccer (or "football," as they call it in Great Britain). The match was between two English professional squads. One team scored a goal the usual way, but the game didn't count. In a rematch between the two squads, that team scored a goal again—in a very *unusual* way. This time, it counted.

Confused? It's all part of a tale about, as one team manager put it, "the right and proper thing to do."

The originally scheduled game was between two rivals, the Leicester City Foxes and the Nottingham Forest Reds. At halftime, Nottingham had a 1–0 lead. Then something frightening happened. Clive Clarke, a 27-year-old Leicester City defender, had a heart attack. "I came down the tunnel at halftime feeling a little bit dizzy, light-headed. I went into the changing room, sat down, and the next thing I knew I woke up in the back

WISE WORDS

"The thing about football—the important thing about football— is that it is not just about football."

—Terry Pratchett, English writer and soccer fan

of an ambulance," Clarke later recalled. "I was lucky I had good people around me who acted very quickly and saved my life."

Clarke would never play another match. He retired from professional football a few months later. But the Leicester and Nottingham teams turned a sad and scary event into an example of respect and fair play. When Clarke got sick, Nottingham was leading 1–0. They had a shot at beating their rivals. Even so, the team agreed without hesitation to cancel the game. "Football is secondary to human issues," said Mark Arthur, Nottingham's chief executive. "Once we found out the seriousness of Clive's situation we went straight to the referee and told him we would do whatever was right by Leicester."

But Leicester also wanted to do right by Nottingham. The teams decided to replay the game two weeks later. Leicester's mission: Give Nottingham its goal back. "The idea came from the whole club," said Leicester team chairman Milan Mandarić. "We all like to win games, but morality and fairness are also important."

When the game began, a Leicester player tapped the ball to the Nottingham goalkeeper, Paul Smith. Smith was standing at midfield. "Paul Smith's taking the kickoff! Now what is going on here?" the announcer wondered. It isn't surprising that he was confused. Because on the field, Smith's red-shirted Leicester opponents were simply clearing the way for him. He had a clear path to dribble downfield. "Paul Smith is being allowed to run forward, and he's going to score!" Just before Smith kicked the ball into the goal, the opposing goaltender offered him a high-five. "What a sporting gesture that is from Leicester City!" the announcer marveled.

It was 1–0 Nottingham again, just as it had been when the previous game was cancelled. Although Leicester wound up winning 3–2, Nottingham's manager, Colin Calderwood, put it best. He said, "I would like to think that football in general has come out of the game as the winner."

THE CONCESSION

SEPTEMBER 20, 1969 • SOUTHPORT, ENGLAND

Every other year, a team of the best professional golfers from the United States competes against a group
of top European golfers. Dating back to 1927, the event
is called the Ryder Cup Matches. In 1969, the competition was between American and British players. The
U.S. team had won 14 of the previous 18 Ryder Cups.
When they arrived at England's famous Royal Birkdale
Golf Club, they were heavily favored to win again.

During the first two days of the three-day event,
pairs from both teams played against each other.
After each match, the winning side got a team point.
If there was a tie, each team received half a point. The
Americans and the Brits recorded eight points apiece.
The last day of competition featured singles (one-on-
one) competition. After the first seven matches, the
two teams were still tied. They each had 15½ points.

The day's closing match featured 29-year-old American Jack Nicklaus (who would go on to become the most successful player in golf history) against 50-year-old British star Tony Jacklin. And the theme continued. After the first 15 holes, the match was *still* all-square. Tied up. Nicklaus made a birdie (one under par) on the 16th hole, taking the lead by one point. Then Jacklin made an amazing 50-foot putt on

A GOOD GOLFER

Mount Gilead High School sophomore golfer Adam Van Houten had played the last hole. He had won the 2005 Division II high school state championship in Columbus, Ohio. At least, that's what he thought. Then, after signing his scorecard, he realized that his playing partner had recorded his score on one hole as a five. But he had really taken six strokes. It wouldn't influence the order of finishers in the tournament. It did affect Van Houten's conscience, though. Even though signing an incorrect scorecard meant automatic disqualification, he reported the error. The act lost him the tournament and his state title. However, it earned him the Ohio High School Athletic Association Ethics and Integrity Award.

the 17th green to win the hole and tie the match once more. The whole Ryder Cup competition would come down to the 18th and final hole.

After three shots each, Nicklaus stood over a putt about five feet from the hole. Jacklin's ball was closer, only two feet from the cup. With the Ryder Cup on the line, Nicklaus took his stroke. The ball fell right into the hole. Now the U.S. team was guaranteed at *least* a tie in the overall Ryder Cup point standings. And because the Americans were the defending champions, a tie meant that they would retain the Ryder Cup trophy for another two years.

Jacklin still had a two-foot putt to make. He knew that if he missed—in front of thousands of spectators—the Americans would win outright. Nicklaus knew it, too. He quickly walked up to Jacklin's ball marker, reached down and picked it up. He was conceding the putt. This concession meant that he was agreeing to credit Jacklin with making the shot. "I don't think you would have missed that, Tony," he told Jacklin, "but I didn't want to give you the chance." The two men shook hands. For the first time in its 42-year history, the Ryder Cup ended in a 16–16 tie.

Nicklaus's gesture is considered one of the great acts of sportsmanship in golf history. It was also the beginning of a long friendship between the two men.

In fact, more than 30 years later, Nicklaus and Jacklin designed a golf course in Florida together.
They called it the Concession Golf Club.

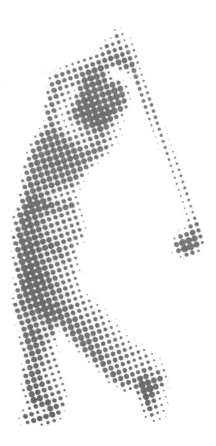

SNOW ANGEL

FEBRUARY 14, 2006 • TURIN, ITALY

It was Sara Renner's dream to win a medal at the Olympic Games. It had been her dream almost since she was born—in a town called Golden.

The Canadian cross-country skier got her first Olympic experience in 1998. That year she competed at the Winter Games in Nagano, Japan. But she finished far behind the medal winners. Not long afterward, she was diagnosed with a condition called Graves' disease. She had to have her thyroid removed. Still, her dreams remained. She came back to compete in the 2002 Olympics in Salt Lake City, Utah. This time, she competed in four events. Her highest finish was eighth place. Renner vowed to return once more. In 2006, she headed to Turin, Italy, with her skis, her poles, and her mission to win a medal.

At the Turin Olympics, Renner's best chance at a gold was the women's team sprint competition.

During the final race, she started strong. But then a competitor accidentally stepped on one of Renner's poles, breaking it. Renner wobbled forward for a few moments. But it was a bit like trying to fly with a broken wing. In a 17-minute race, every second counted. Renner despaired as skiers from Finland, Sweden, and Norway glided past her.

TRUE SPIRIT

Eugenio Monti was one of the finest bobsledders in history. The Italian won six Olympic medals, including two golds. But he is also well-known for an act of generosity at the 1964 Winter Games in Austria. When he heard that the British two-man bobsled team had a broken bolt on their sled, Monti lent them a bolt from his. Later, he and his mechanics fixed a Canadian team's damaged sled axle. The Brits and the Canadians won gold medals, while Monti took home bronzes. But Monti won something else for his sportsmanlike actions. He became the first athlete to receive the International Olympic Committee's Pierre de Coubertin medal. This award is named after the founder of the modern Olympic Games. It is also known as the True Spirit of Sportsmanship medal.

Then a man appeared by the course. He handed Renner a pole. She grabbed it and continued on.

Renner described him as "my mystery man," but it turned out to be no mystery at all. The helpful man was Bjørnar Håkensmoen. He was the Norwegian cross-country skiing coach. Cross-country skiing is one form of Nordic skiing, which is Norway's national sport. This would be Håkensmoen's last Olympic Games. Like Renner, he desperately hoped his team would return home with a medal. But when he saw Renner in trouble, he didn't hesitate. "Winning is not everything in sport," he later explained. "What win is that, if you achieve your goal but don't help somebody when you should have helped them?"

Renner's new pole was longer than her old one, but it was a whole lot better than a broken pole. She charged forward to a silver medal with teammate Beckie Scott. The two skiers hugged and joyfully collapsed into the snow.

The Norwegians finished fourth. Håkensmoen's skiers just missed taking a medal home, but the coach had no regrets. "How can you be proud of a medal if you win when someone else's equipment is not working?" he asked. The people of his country were even prouder of his behavior. And Canadians? They treated him like an Olympic hero, sending flowers and letters to the Norwegian embassy in Canada. One maple-sugar farmer even started a program called Project Maple Syrup, dedicated to shipping Canada's tasty treasure over to Norway. In all, more than five tons of syrup arrived in Håkensmoen's home country!

Renner went on to win a bronze medal at the 2010 Olympics in Vancouver, Canada. But before that, she gave Håkensmoen a gift and a note thanking him for his help during that February 14 race. Renner said, "He was my valentine."

TRADING PLACES

MAY 23, 2008 • PASCO, WASHINGTON, UNITED STATES

At the 2008 Washington State Class 4A Track and Field Championship, Nicole Cochran had just finished the 3,200-meter race. The defending champion thought she had won. After all, Cochran—a senior at Bellarmine Prep—seemed to have finished first by more than three seconds. But then her coach was called to the officials' tent. The officials said that Cochran had stepped outside of her lane during one of the turns. Cochran knew she hadn't done it, but the ruling was final. She was going to be disqualified.

Almost everybody, including the other runners, believed the judge had made a mistake. In fact, a video of the race later proved it. Still, the title was awarded to the runner-up, Andrea Nelson from Shadle Park High.

Nelson wasn't happy about it. In fact, she was upset. She had been running in the lane next to

51

Cochran's, and she knew Cochran had run a clean race. "That's not how I wanted to win state," said Nelson. "It wasn't fair. She deserved it. She totally crushed everybody." So as the eight top finishers took their places on the podium to receive their medals, Nelson made a decision. She stepped off the podium, walked over to Cochran, and placed the first-place medal around her neck. "It's your medal," she said.

SPORTING SWITCH

At the 1928 Summer Olympics held in the Netherlands, it was almost time for the finals of the 110-meter hurdles. In the semifinals, South African George Weightman-Smith had set a world record of 14.6 seconds. Now he, along with his fellow finalists, nervously awaited the draw for lanes in the final race. No one wanted the inside lane, which had been badly chewed up by rain and overuse. Another South African, Syd Atkinson, had lost the Olympic finals by only inches four years earlier. Atkinson drew the unwanted lane. He was deeply disappointed. So Weightman-Smith walked over to his teammate and offered to switch lanes. Atkinson refused, but his teammate insisted. Atkinson went on to win the gold. Weightman-Smith sloshed home in fifth place.

Cochran was moved by the gesture. "I was pretty flabbergasted," she remembered. The other runners were inspired, too. The second-place finisher gave her medal to Nelson. Then the third-place finisher gave her medal to the second-place runner, and so on down the line. Finally, a girl named Lyndy Davis from Monroe High School gave her eighth-place medal away. That meant she wouldn't be receiving one at all. "It gave me chills," said Cochran. "It shows how much respect distance runners have for each other."

Cochran competed in two more events, including the 800-meter race. She finished in eighth place. Afterward, she found Lyndy Davis and gave her the eighth-place medal. "After what she had done, I didn't want her to go home from the meet her senior year without a medal," said Cochran. Then, 10 days after the competition, officials decided the original ruling had been wrong. Cochran was formally named the 3,200-meter champ. "Even though I am now the state champion," said Cochran, who went on to run track at Harvard University, "the thing I will remember most from that weekend is the sportsmanship displayed by those girls who didn't need anyone to tell them the right thing to do." Or as her coach Matt Ellis put it, "we can all learn from what those girls did."

MAKING A POINT

AUGUST 24, 1958 • PORTO, PORTUGAL

For many years, when British policemen stopped motorists for driving too fast, they would ask a common question: "Who do you think you are? Stirling Moss?" The British racecar driver's name was synonymous with speed.

The racing career of Sir Stirling Moss (he was knighted for his service to sports) lasted from 1948 to 1962. He competed in more than 500 races in many countries. The cars he raced included Porsches, Jaguars, Ferraris, and Maseratis. A member of the International Motorsports Hall of Fame, Moss won more than 200 races. But for all his accomplishments, he never finished as the top driver in the Formula One Grand Prix circuit. In fact, he has been described as the greatest driver never to win the World Championship.

There was a time when he *could* have won it. But Moss chose to be a world-class sportsman instead.

Heading into the Portuguese Grand Prix in 1958, Moss was second in the points standings. He trailed only his rival, Mike Hawthorn. That August race took place on a tricky street course. It had some slippery sections, and they were even more slippery that day because of earlier rain. For much of the day, Moss and Hawthorn battled back and forth for the lead. The 50,000 fans looked on breathlessly. In the end, when the checkered flag was waved, Moss came in first. His time was just over 2 hours and 11 minutes, more than five minutes ahead of second-place Hawthorn. That meant that he earned eight points, pulling to within five total points of Hawthorn's total.

Hawthorn's season total included seven points from that slippery race. He earned six for his second-place finish. He also got an extra point for making the fastest lap.

But questions followed the race. At one point, Hawthorn had spun off the slick road. He pushed his Ferrari back toward the course, jammed it into gear, and jumped in. His car was facing the wrong way on a footpath, but he swung around to the road and kept racing. Afterward, observers told race officials that Hawthorn had broken the rules by driving a few yards in the wrong direction. Those reports could mean that

WHEN A TIE IS A WIN

British jockey Peter Scudamore was leading the points race for the National Hunt Jockeys Championship in 1982. Then he suffered a season-ending injury. His closest rival in the horseracing circuit, John Francome, had won three straight titles. When he tied Scudamore's point total, he seemed poised to win a fourth in a row. But instead, he decided then to stop racing for the rest of the season. He said that his decision was based on respect for his opponent. Francome felt Scudamore deserved something to show for such a fine season. The two riders shared the title of Champion Jockey that year.

he would be disqualified and stripped of the seven points he'd won in the race.

But Stirling Moss had witnessed the moment, too. He came to Hawthorn's defense. Moss told the race officials that his fellow Englishman had done nothing wrong. He insisted that the footpath did not constitute "the wrong way of the circuit" (as the rules stated). Besides, he added, there had been no danger to any other competitors, so Hawthorn should not be penalized. After listening to Moss's explanation, the officials agreed to let Hawthorn's second-place finish stand.

By the end of the year, Moss had won 4 of the 11 Grand Prix races. That was more than any other driver. But Hawthorn had finished first once and second five times. When all the points were tallied, Moss, who had placed second in Grand Prix points three years in a row, came in second again—one point behind Hawthorn.

"YOU'RE GOING TO MISS THEM"

FEBRUARY 14, 2009 • MILWAUKEE, WISCONSIN, UNITED STATES

It had been a long night. The DeKalb High School boys' basketball team had travelled for two-and-a-half hours by bus from Illinois to reach the gym of their opponent, Milwaukee Madison High in Wisconsin. Then the game had been delayed for a tragic reason. Just hours earlier, the mother of Johntel Franklin, Milwaukee Madison's senior co-captain, had died suddenly. Several of Franklin's teammates had been at the hospital with him when the family decided to turn off his mother's life support. Naturally, Franklin was crushed.

Milwaukee's coach, Aaron Womack Jr., decided to cancel the evening's basketball game. But somebody talked him out of it. That somebody was Franklin. He said he wanted the team to play.

WISE WORDS

"I think sportsmanship is knowing that it is a game, that we are only as a good as our opponents, and whether you win or lose, to always give 100 percent."

—Sue Wicks, former WNBA basketball player

The game started late, and only eight Milwaukee players were in uniform. The contest was close throughout the first quarter. Then, early in the second quarter, Franklin himself appeared. He had come directly from the hospital to root for his teammates. They called a timeout and hugged their grieving friend. Several fans came out of the crowd to do the same.

When the game resumed, Coach Womack invited Franklin to sit on the bench. Franklin shook his head. "No," he said. "I want to play."

But there was a problem. The coach hadn't included Franklin on the team's pregame roster. If he put him in the game now, a technical foul had to be called. The other team would get two free throws. Coach Womack didn't hesitate. He was more than willing to pay that price for Franklin's sake—even though the game was close.

However, DeKalb's coach, Dave Rohlman, said his team wouldn't take the free throws. He told the referees to forget about it. "We're not taking it." He said it over and over again. The argument went on for several minutes. But the referees insisted. Rules were rules. So Coach Rohlman asked for a volunteer. Darius McNeal, DeKalb's senior captain, raised his hand. As he walked toward the free throw line, his coach said something most players wouldn't expect to hear: "You realize you're going to miss them, don't you?"

McNeal nodded. He stood at the line, dribbled a couple of times, and threw the ball—threw it about two feet, that is. His second shot was even worse. In fact, it was hardly even a shot. McNeal pretty much just dropped the ball.

When the Milwaukee players realized what was happening, they stood up and turned toward the DeKalb bench. The whole team started clapping. Soon, everyone in the gym was applauding the visiting team. After the game, before the two teams went out for pizza and sodas together, McNeal told a reporter, "I did it for the guy who lost his mom. It was the right thing to do."

In the end, Milwaukee Madison won the game. Franklin even scored 10 points. But the DeKalb players didn't feel like losers. "This is something our kids will hold for a lifetime," said their coach. "They may not remember our record 20 years from now, but they'll remember what happened in the gym that night."

ICE HOCKEY

HATS OFF

DECEMBER 11, 2011 • WASHINGTON, D.C., UNITED STATES

The Washington Capitals were ahead of the visiting Toronto Maple Leafs 3–2 with less than two minutes left in the game. The main reason for the lead? Capitals defenseman Dennis Wideman. He had contributed to all three goals, scoring twice and assisting on a third. His first goal had been on a wrist shot from in front of the net in the first period of play.

"Wideman!" the television announcer shouted.

His second goal had come early in the second period, giving Washington a 2–0 lead. "Wideman uncorks one," said the announcer, as the defenseman fired a slap shot from just in front of the blue line. "He scores!"

Two goals in a game is a rare feat for a defenseman. It was especially rare for Wideman. In his 11 years in the National Hockey League, he had never recorded more than 13 goals in an entire *season*. If he scored a third goal tonight, his performance would be remarkable for another reason, too. It would give him a "hat trick," as three goals in one game are known in hockey, soccer, and a few other sports. No Washington defenseman had earned a hat trick in almost 12 years.

With just a minute and 19 seconds left to play, Wideman took a pass from a teammate at the top of the left faceoff circle. Another Washington teammate, Brooks Laich, stood in front of the Toronto goaltender. It was a perfect chance for Wideman to make team history. He drew his stick back and sent a slap shot toward the goal. "Wideman fires," said the announcer. "Scores!" In the blink of an eye, the puck was in the back of the net.

A horn sounded. The Capitals players raised their arms in triumph and skated over to hug and high-five their teammate. The Washington home crowd cheered and began to toss their hats onto the ice, a unique hockey tradition.

But right after the game, Wideman told reporters that his third goal shouldn't count toward a hat trick. "The third one went off Brooksie. So I'm pretty sure that one's going to come back," he said. What Wideman meant was that he hadn't made the goal alone. And that meant it wouldn't count toward a hat

WAVE OF HONESTY

During a California surfing event in November 2011, professional surfer Kelly Slater was declared the world champion. It seemed as though he had won his 11th world title. But later he saw a comment while surfing the Internet. An observer had noticed that, mathematically, Slater actually hadn't clinched that 11th title *quite* yet. Slater did the math himself and agreed. He actually needed to win one more heat of a surfing competition to earn the title of world champion. So he reported the mistake to officials. "Your parents always tell you," he explained, "honesty is the best policy." Two days later, in a competition at San Francisco's Ocean Beach, Slater earned enough points to win the title for real.

trick. Wideman said the puck had bounced off teammate Brooks Laich's leg before going into the net. It
was hard to know for sure if he was right, even after
viewing the instant replay. Still, Wideman insisted that
the league should review it carefully. He'd never had a
hat trick before, not in any of his 481 NHL games. And,
he added, "Still haven't had one."

The next day, NHL officials reviewed the play. They
agreed with Wideman. The puck had, indeed,
bounced off of his teammate. Wideman would be
credited with an assist instead. No hat trick.

Of course, Wideman would have loved to
have scored a hat trick. But as he put it, "If
you get one, you want it to be honest. You
don't want a cheap one." After the NHL's
decision was made public, he was asked
why he had chosen postgame honesty.
"Good karma," he explained.
"Good karma."

MARATHON PERSPECTIVE

AUGUST 29, 2004 •ATHENS, GREECE

In the very first modern Olympic Games in Athens, Greece, in 1896, the marathon was the main event. A Greek runner named Spyridon Louis thrilled the home crowd by winning the race, finishing a full seven minutes ahead of his closest competitor. The third-place finisher was another Greek runner named Spyridon Belokas. However, another runner later said that the bronze-winning Belokas had cheated. He had actually ridden in a carriage for part of the race!

When the Summer Olympics returned to Athens in 2004, controversy hit the marathon again. But this time, the bad behavior was turned into a positive by three men who showed courage, class, and generosity.

With about four miles left in the 26.2-mile competition, it looked like 35-year-old Vanderlei de Lima had the race well in hand. The Brazilian runner had been the fastest marathoner at both the 1999 and 2003 Pan-American Games. Now he had a good lead over a pack of runners, and he was still looking strong. Suddenly, a man wearing a kilt and a beret charged onto the course. He pushed de Lima into the crowd. Everyone was stunned—especially the runner. "I was completely concentrating on the race, and there was no way I could defend myself," explained de Lima. "I can't say whether I would have won the gold medal or not," he went on. "But it certainly caused me a lot of trouble."

He recovered, but not completely. The attack cost him as much as 10 to 20 seconds. Even more damaging, it completely disrupted his focus and rhythm. Soon, Italian runner Stefano Baldini passed de Lima. Baldini went on to win the gold. Then American Meb Keflezighi ran by. De Lima wound up in third place, 77 seconds behind the Olympic champion.

At first, the event was considered a low point of the 2004 Olympics. But the awful actions of one man came to be overshadowed by the inspiring responses of three others. First, there was the spectator who immediately came to de Lima's aid. This unidentified man helped de Lima get away from the attacker (who was arrested).

Then there was de Lima himself. At the end of the race, thousands cheered him as he ran into the same stadium that had been the site of the first marathon finish line 108 years earlier. He responded by spreading his arms wide, smiling broadly, and weaving from side to side in a little victory dance. "My dream was an Olympic medal," he said the following day. He added that his happiness at winning the bronze was

PRECIOUS MEDALS

At the 1936 Summer Olympics in Berlin, Germany, American Earle Meadows finished first in the pole vault. Then Japanese teammates Shuhei Nishida and Sueo Oe, who had cleared the same height as each other, were told to compete for second and third place. But instead of continuing their "vault-off," the two friends simply decided that it didn't matter which of them won. One was given a silver medal, and the other a bronze. When they arrived back home in Japan, they visited a jeweler and asked him to cut both medals in half. Next they had the different halves fused together. In the end, each man had a medal that was half silver and half bronze. Nishida and Oe called it a Medal of Friendship.

"greater than any feeling of bitterness that could have stayed with me." He was later awarded the Pierre de Coubertin medal in recognition of his "exceptional demonstration of fair play and Olympic values."

And finally, a third man rose above the troubling event. One of de Lima's fellow Brazilian Olympians wanted to give him something. Nearly a year later, on national television in Brazil, gold-medal-winning beach volleyball player Emanuel Rego offered his prize to de Lima. The runner was touched, but he promptly returned the gift. "I can't accept Emanuel's medal," he said. "I'm happy with mine. It's bronze, but means gold."

FIRST-CLASS AID

SEPTEMBER 16, 2011 • LAKEVILLE, MINNESOTA, UNITED STATES

There were 260 runners besides Mark Paulauskas in the Applejack Invite boys' cross-country race. Only one stopped to help him.

Paulauskas was a freshman runner for Lakeville South High School, located in a suburb of Minneapolis, Minnesota. Less than a kilometer into the five-kilometer race that September day, he'd been injured. Many runners wear pointed metal spikes on their shoes to get better traction. As Paulauskas turned a corner along the course, he was accidentally spiked by a competitor's shoe. The spike opened up a nasty gash in his ankle. Paulauskas crumpled to the ground. He crawled from the path of the other runners and huddled against a fence. His ankle was bleeding badly.

Many runners passed him by. Maybe they were so engrossin the race that they didn't see him. Perhaps they didn't realize how serious his injury was. Maybe, for some of them, a good race time was more important than good sportsmanship. But then Josh Ripley, a junior from Andover High School, came running by. He saw that Paulauskas was bleeding and holding his ankle.

After the accident, Paulauskas would eventually take a trip to the emergency room, where he needed 20 stitches to close the wound. He also needed a walking boot to protect the area and keep the stitches in

LAST BUT NOT LEAST

In 2011, the rowing team of Nick Mead and James Konopka had high hopes. They were competing for Episcopal Academy at the Head of the Schuylkill race in Philadelphia. Mead and Konopka had a good chance at winning the Under-17 Doubles title. But the boys actually finished at the back of the pack. Why? Because during the race they stopped to rescue a couple of competitors whose boat had turned over. Afterward, their coach, Rob Maier, said, "We are all training to win races against each other, but the culture on the river is much more cooperative than combative. It looks like that rubbed off on our rowers."

place. All that came later. When the accident happened, Paulauskas was in no condition to walk and get help.

That's where Ripley came in. "I didn't think about my race. I knew I needed to stop and help him," Ripley recalled. "It was something I would expect my other teammates to do."

At 6-foot-5 and 185 pounds, Josh was a foot taller and nearly 85 pounds heavier than Paulauskas. Without a word, he simply lifted him and began carrying the injured runner back toward safety. As Paulauskas later described it, "He just scooped me up, and I was like, whoa." Ripley had never met Paulauskas, but he tried to calm down the freshman runner. "It's going to be okay," he told him. "I'm going to get you to your coaches."

Meanwhile, Ripley's coach, Scott Clark, was waiting for his runner to pass by. And waiting. And waiting. *What's going on?* he wondered. *Why is he so far back?* "Then I see Josh," he recalled. "He's got the kid in his arms."

Carrying Paulauskas, Ripley jogged about half a mile to an area of the course where he could get help. Ripley dropped Paulauskas off, turned around, and kept running. He had a race to finish. Although by then he was dead last in the field, he made up for lost time. Ripley passed 50 runners along the course, finishing in 211th place. Among those at the finish line were Paulauskas's coach and teammates. They greeted Ripley with cheers and applause so loud it was as if he had set a new course record.

Paulauskas later talked about how "incredibly grateful" he was for Ripley's help. Paulauskas's father called it a "selfless act of compassion, kindness, and sportsmanship." But Ripley only shrugged. "I'm nothing special," he said. "I was just in the right place at the right time."

"A REAL CHAMPION"

MAY 20, 2000 • COLORADO SPRINGS, COLORADO, UNITED STATES

Sometimes best friends are rivals. And sometimes competition is no match for friendship.

It was the 2000 U.S. Olympic team trials in the Korean martial art of tae kwon do. In Colorado Springs, Colorado, the finals of the women's flyweight division pitted 18-year-old Kay Poe against 20-year-old Esther Kim. Poe and Kim shared the hometown of Houston, Texas. And the two had been best friends since meeting at a Halloween party more than a decade earlier. "I think of her more as a sister," said Poe. "We've grown up together, and we always push each other and help each other out the best we can." However, only the winner of their final match could compete at the Summer Olympics in Sydney, Australia.

The two black belts were evenly matched. But because Poe had won a gold medal at the World Cup Championships two years earlier, she was ranked higher. As the top-ranked flyweight in the world, she was a good bet to win an Olympic medal. There was a problem, though. In the final seconds of her semifinal match earlier that day, Poe had banged knees with her opponent. She had a dislocated kneecap. Although she still won the match, her coach had to carry her from the mat afterward. (Her coach, by the way, was Esther Kim's father, Jin Won Kim.) Poe's next bout—against her best friend—was less than an hour away.

Kim made her way to Poe, who was writhing in pain. Kim helped her friend ice her knee, but it was badly swollen. Kim knew Poe couldn't compete. Even if they did fight, Kim was afraid that Poe might suffer a career-threatening injury, especially because tae kwon do uses many kicking moves. It also encourages discipline, unselfishness, and sacrifice.

When Kim saw that Poe couldn't even stand, she blurted out, "What if I just bow down to you when we get in the ring?" Kim was offering to let Poe win automatically.

Poe shook her head. "We have to fight."

"Don't argue," Kim replied.

The time came for the match to begin. Kim and her father carried Poe to the mat. Then Kim shocked the crowed. She bowed to Poe, giving up her own chance for a spot in the Olympics so that her higher-ranked friend could go instead. "Never in a million years did I think something like this would happen," Poe later said. "It's such a wonderful gift she gave me."

Kim had always dreamed of competing in the Olympics, and she would never qualify for another

BROTHERLY LOVE

At the 1900 Olympic Games in Paris, France, English tennis player Reginald Doherty and his younger brother Laurence won the doubles tennis title. The two were known by nicknames—Reggie and Laurie. Sometimes Laurence was also called "Little Do." In the singles tournament, the brothers were scheduled to play against each other in the semifinals. Reggie was the better player at the time. He had won at the Wimbledon Championships four years in a row. But he refused to compete against his brother. So he withdrew, and "Little Do" went on to win the title. Eighty years later, they were inducted into the International Tennis Hall of Fame—together.

one. But for her act of selflessness, she received a Citizenship Through Sports Award. And when Juan Antonio Samaranch, president of the International Olympic Committee, heard the story, he offered Kim an all-expenses-paid trip to Australia to watch her best friend compete. (Poe wound up falling short of a medal.)

"Kay has always fought with all her heart," Kim explained. "I wasn't throwing my dreams away, I was handing them to Kay." She added, "Even though I didn't have the gold medal around me, for the first time in my life, I felt like a real champion."

RECORD RE-SET

At age 17, Nate Haasis entered the final game of his senior year. He was also close to entering the record books. Haasis was the quarterback at Springfield Southeast High School in Illinois. And he needed just 222 passing yards to break the all-time Central State Eight Conference record. However, as the game against Cahokia High neared its end, it looked like he was going to fall just 29 yards short.

With only 30 seconds left, Cahokia had the ball and a 16-point lead. It didn't seem as though the record of 4,998 career passing yards, set five years earlier, was going to fall that day. Then Haasis's coach, Neal Taylor, called a timeout. He walked to midfield, huddled with the opposing coach for a moment, and returned to the sideline. Suddenly, a football game that seemed all but over became a bit . . . strange. Although the quarterback didn't know it, the coaches had come up with a plan.

When play started again, the Springfield defenders didn't do much defending at all. Cahokia easily scored a 28-yard touchdown. Then they purposely sent a kickoff out of bounds. With eight seconds left, Springfield's offense took the field. Coach Taylor had figured out exactly how many yards Haasis needed to break the record. He walked to a specific spot on the sideline. When Haasis took the game's final snap, he saw that the Cahokia players didn't seem to be paying

RECORDS AND RESPECT

Lisa Helmers was a star on the girls' basketball team at Corona del Sol High School in Tempe, Arizona. In 2005, she set her school's single-game scoring record. Helmers sank 41 points against Shadow Mountain High School in Phoenix. When Corona coach Pat Reed mentioned it on the sidelines, a Shadow Mountain official overheard her. The official shared the information with the opposing coach, Gerrard Carmichael. Although the game was still going, Carmichael stopped play and presented Helmers with a game ball. "We were shocked. It was a precious moment for Lisa," said Reed afterward. "Some say there isn't much sportsmanship anymore, but that shows that there is."

much attention. "That's when I knew something was up," he said later.

Haasis threw a five-yard pass to Springfield receiver Jacque Robinson. Robinson was so open, as one writer later joked, "he must think his deodorant has failed." Robinson ran another 32 yards with the ball—to where his coach was standing. With the 37-yard gain, Haasis reached 5,006 passing yards. That was a new conference record. It made him only the 12th quarterback in Illinois high school history to surpass 5,000 yards.

Haasis's coach, who had known his quarterback since the seventh grade, was a good man with good intentions. But Haasis was uncomfortable with breaking the record this way. "I kept thinking of the guy who had the record before me," he said. "I mean, his teammates fought for every yard he got. And then I get mine this way? It just seemed wrong."

Three days later, Haasis made it right. He wrote a letter to the president of the athletic conference. In the letter, he said, "It is my belief that the directions given to us in the final seconds of this game were made in 'the heat of battle' and do not represent the values of the athletes of the Southeast football team." Haasis went on, "In respect to my teammates, and past and present football players of the Central State

Eight, it is my hope that this pass is omitted from any conference records."

The conference granted Haasis's request. Griff Jurgens, whose passing mark Haasis had apparently broken (and then un-broken), told reporters he had "the utmost respect for him." Plus, Haasis discovered that his own self-respect mattered more than any record. "Right away, I felt better," he said. "I wanted the record, but I didn't want it in the way I got it. So in that sense, it wasn't a hard decision at all."

ACE OF HEARTS

MAY 4, 2005 • ROME, ITALY

American tennis star Andy Roddick was one point
away from victory. It was the quarterfinals of the
Rome Masters clay court tournament. As the 2003 U.S.
Open champion and former number one player in the
world, Roddick was the top-seeded player in Rome. He
had already won the first set against his quarterfinals
opponent, Spain's Fernando Verdasco. Now he was
up 5–3, 40–love in the second set. It was triple match

point. That meant Roddick had three chances to win a single point and move on to the semifinals.

It was Verdasco's serve. He had already missed on his first attempt. His second serve appeared to land too deep. The line judge called it "out." Double fault. Point for Roddick. The crowd began to applaud. The umpire started to announce Roddick as the winner. Verdasco began to walk to the net to congratulate him. Everybody believed the match was over.

Everybody except Roddick.

Only a few months earlier, he had received the Arthur Ashe Humanitarian of the Year Award for his charity work. That work included creating the Andy Roddick Foundation to help young people at risk. Roddick had also raised money for the survivors of a devastating tsunami in Asia. On the court, however, he was not always known for good sportsmanship. Sometimes he yelled at umpires. He had even smashed balls into the stands in frustration. But on this day, at this moment, Andy Roddick did the right thing.

Because the court was clay, Roddick could see the ball mark from Verdasco's second serve. The line judge thought it had been out, but Roddick noticed that the ball had actually nicked the boundary line. That meant it was officially "in." Roddick said so, pointing out the evidence. The stunned umpire changed his call, giving Verdasco an ace. Still, nobody really thought it would change the outcome of the match. But Verdasco won the next point, and the next, and the next. He wound up winning the set and, eventually, the whole match.

> "Sportsmanship for me is when a guy walks off the court and you really can't tell whether he won or lost, when he carries himself with pride either way."
>
> —Jim Courier, four-time Grand Slam tennis champion

As a result of this moment of honesty, Roddick's name became a symbol of sportsmanship. In his book *The Speed of Trust*, author Stephen M.R. Covey coined a term called "the Roddick Choice." He defined it as "demonstrating integrity even when it is costly."

After the match, Verdasco said, "I have to thank him. He is a great sportsman." But Roddick explained, "I don't think it was anything extraordinary. The umpire would have done the same thing if he came down and looked. I just saved him the trip."

Sportswriter Frank Deford didn't see it that way. He pointed out that Roddick wouldn't have been criticized if he hadn't said anything. Professional athletes often use tactics that aren't completely honest. They pretend to be fouled, or to be hit by a pitch. They stay silent when an umpire or referee makes a bad call. "If Roddick keeps his mouth shut, he wins," wrote Deford. "I don't know about you, but to my mind, if there's still a small place in heaven for athletes, Andy Roddick just got his wings."

SELECTED BIBLIOGRAPHY

Allen, Scott. "10 Acts of Good Sportsmanship." *mentalfloss.com/article/25152/10-acts-good-sportsmanship*. July 9, 2010 (accessed March 30, 2011).

Bamberger, Michael. "My Sportsman: Josh Ripley." *sportsillustrated.cnn.com/2011/magazine/sportsman/11/28/bamberger.ripley*. December 2, 2011 (accessed April 5, 2011).

Dahlberg, Tim. "A Touching Display of Sportsmanship." Associated Press, *The Monterey County Herald*. February 19, 2009.

Deford, Frank. "Game, Set, Ma-----: In Losing a Match, Roddick Became a True Sportsman." *sportsillustrated.cnn.com/2005/writers/frank_deford/05/11/deford.sportsmanship*. May 11, 2005 (accessed April 7, 2011).

Longman, Jere. "Two Athletes, an Injury and a Sacrifice." *The New York Times*. May 25, 2000.

Picker, David. "Quarterback Is Rejecting Mark He Feels Is Tainted." *The New York Times*. November 1, 2003.

Schaap, Jeremy. *Triumph: The Untold Story of Jesse Owens and Hitler's Olympics*. New York: Mariner Books, 2007.

Taylor, Phil. "Precious Medal." *Sports Illustrated*. December 29, 2008.

Vecsey, George. "A Sporting Gesture Touches 'Em All." *The New York Times*. April 30, 2008.

Verducci, Tom. "A Different Kind of Perfect." *Sports Illustrated*. June 14, 2010.

Vogel, Meghan (interviewed by Doug Binder). "Meghan Vogel." *ESPN The Magazine*. November 2012.

Wallechinsky, David. *The Complete Book of the Olympics*. New York: Penguin Books, 1988.

Wise, Mike. "Honorable Move Made in a Snap." *The Washington Post*. February 26, 2006.

INDEX

Interior photo credits: Dot pattern images created by Michelle Lee Lagerroos; page 4: AP Photo/Blake Wolf; page 8: Bettmann/Corbis/AP Images; page 11: based on a photo by Chad Kainz; page 12: Press Association via AP Images; page 15: based on a photo by Chris Parfitt; page 18: based on photos by Dru Bloomfield and © Ariwasabi/Dreamstime.com; page 21: AP Photo/Paul Sancya; page 29: based on a photo by © Cherezoff/Dreamstime.com; page 30: Bettmann/Corbis/AP Images; page 38: Press Association via AP Images; page 45: based on a photo by Neville Wootton; page 46: AP Photo/Frank Gunn/CP; page 50: based on a photo by Szymon Nitka; page 53: based on a photo by © Flynt/Dreamstime.com; page 55: AP Photo; page 58: based on a photo by Tharrin; page 62: AP Photo/Nick Wass; page 66: AP Photos/Koji Sasahara; page 75: based on a photo by Lake Mead NRA Public Affairs; page 76: AP Photo/David J. Phillip; page 80: based on a photo by Dave Pape; page 85: AP Photo/Alastair Grant

ABOUT THE AUTHOR

Brad Herzog is the author of more than 30 books for children, including more than two dozen sports books. He has also published three travel memoirs in addition to a fourth book for adults, *The Sports 100*, which ranks and profiles the 100 most important people in U.S. sports history. For his freelance magazine writing (including *Sports Illustrated* and *Sports Illustrated Kids*), Brad has won three gold medals from the Council for Advancement and Support of Education. Brad travels all over the United States visiting schools as a guest author. His website, **bradherzog.com**, includes information about his other books and about his school visits and presentations. Brad lives on California's Monterey Peninsula with his wife and two sons.

Find great sports stories in all the  books

Encourage enthusiasm for reading and inspire positive character development with these powerful stories that highlight character building in sports. Each book features a wide variety of historical and contemporary stories of male and female athletes from around the world. The Count on Me: Sports series demonstrates the power and inspiration of true character. For ages 8–13. *Softcover; 104–112 pp.; 2-color; B&W photos; 5⅛" x 7"*

Interested in purchasing multiple quantities and receiving volume discounts? Contact edsales@freespirit.com or call 1.800.735.7323 and ask for Education Sales.

Many Free Spirit authors are available for speaking engagements, workshops, and keynotes. Contact speakers@freespirit.com or call 1.800.735.7323.

www.freespirit.com